The Quest to Digest

Mary K. Corcoran

Illustrated by Jef Czekaj

ini Charlesbridge

ARE YOU HUNGRY?

To Dad, Mom, Michael and his family, and the Designer of the digestive system—M. K. C.

In memory of Antoinette Konior, who loved to cook almost as much as we loved to eat her food—J. C.

Published by Charlesbridge
85 Main Street
Watertown, MA 02472
(617) 926-0329
www.charlesbridge.com

Library of Congress Cataloging-in-Publication Data
Corcoran, Mary K.
   The quest to digest / Mary K. Corcoran ; illustrated by Jef Czekaj.
      p. cm.
   Summary: "A humorous but factual look at the human digestion process. Includes glossary"—Provided by publisher.
   ISBN-13: 978-1-57091-664-9; ISBN-10: 1-57091-664-0 (reinforced for library use)
   ISBN-13: 978-1-57091-665-6; ISBN-10: 1-57091-665-9 (softcover)
1. Digestion—Juvenile literature. 2. Gastrointestinal system—Juvenile literature. I. Czekaj, Jef. II. Title.
QP145.C835 2006
612.3—dc22   2005019622

Printed in China
(hc) 10 9 8 7 6 5 4 3 2 1
(sc) 10 9 8 7 6 5 4 3 2 1

Line art drawn in ink on bristol and then scanned and
   colored on an Apple iBook using Adobe Photoshop 6.0
Display type set in Ogre and text type set in Monotype's Centaur
Printed and bound by Jade Productions
Production supervision by Brian G. Walker
Designed by Susan Mallory Sherman and Martha MacLeod Sikkema

Well, before you take a
bite out of that apple,
ask yourself, *Why is
food so important?*
Sure, you eat food
when you're
hungry, but
what does food
do for you?

That's easy. Food is your fuel. Your body gets energy from food—energy to:

breathe

walk

talk

run

blink

eat

stay alive!

Your whole body uses the goodies that are in food, like vitamins, proteins, and fats. These good things, called nutrients, give you energy and nourishment.

In order for your body to get this energy, the food must be broken down into smaller and smaller pieces—small enough so your body's cells can use them. To do this, food must go on a quest—

A Quest to Digest!

Chew on This

Believe it or not, there are many organs, or body parts, that help in the digestion process. Let's start with your mouth—the place where digestion begins. It's pretty obvious what is happening there. Your teeth help tear food into small parts. Now, to brush up on teeth, you have different types that do different jobs. To bite into an apple, you use your front teeth, called incisors. Your pointy canine teeth tear the apple, while your molars grind it up with their flat surfaces.

Food must be small enough for you to swallow it correctly. That's why your mom always says, "Chew your food well." It's true: you should chew and chew and chew. . . .

Open Wide

What else is in your mouth besides teeth? Your tongue helps you chew and swallow. And don't forget about saliva, or spit. That's the watery liquid made by the salivary glands, which empty saliva into your mouth through tiny ducts or tubes. You'd be surprised what's in that stuff.

Saliva contains water and enzymes, special "helper proteins" that chemically break down foods called carbohydrates, which are starches and sugars. Saliva also has mucus in it—that slimy, gooey stuff that's in your nose! It sounds yucky, but mucus helps food slide down your throat. Once it is physically broken down by your teeth, food mixes with saliva and forms a package called a bolus.

I SMELL FOOD! START DROOLING, TROOPS!

YES, SIR!

YOUR BRAIN

YOUR SALIVARY GLANDS

You may think saliva is gross, but it's really great to salivate. You don't even have to think about salivating; your body does it for you. You could smell food or even just think about it, and your brain kicks into action, telling the salivary glands to make saliva. Saliva also buddies up with your taste buds so you can taste food. It even helps to keep your mouth clean by getting rid of leftover food particles and some of the bacteria in your mouth. I bet you thought only toothpaste could do that.

It's a Long Road

Gulp . . . you just swallowed some apple. Now, where did that bolus go? It's moving from your pharynx into your esophagus, or "food tube," which is about 10 inches long. A cool little flap, called the epiglottis, covers your trachea at this point, so that food goes to the esophagus and not down the trachea. Food in the trachea causes us to cough or choke. So, good job, epiglottis.

GO TWO INCHES AND THEN MAKE A RIGHT AT THE TRACHEA.

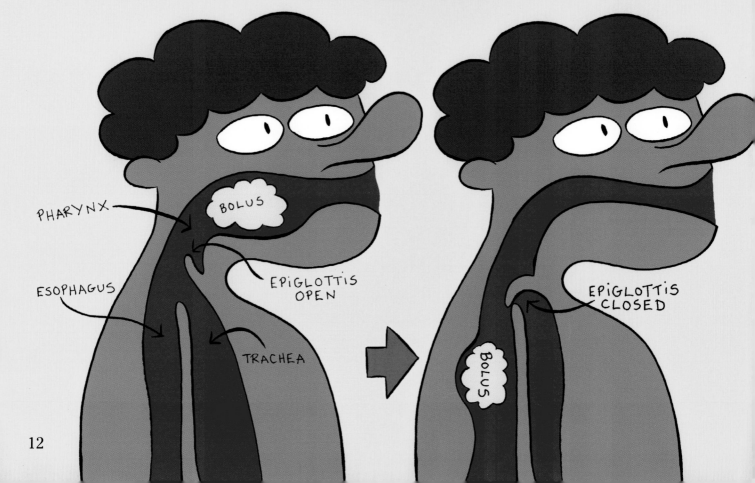

PHARYNX

BOLUS

ESOPHAGUS

EPIGLOTTIS OPEN

TRACHEA

EPIGLOTTIS CLOSED

BOLUS

There's something else hanging around that helps you. . . . It's your uvula. That's the little thing that hangs down in the back of your throat. Open your mouth and look—you can see it. Your soft palate—the roof of your mouth near your uvula—works with your uvula to cover the opening to your nasal passages when you swallow. This way, food can't go up the wrong way into your nose.

Give Me a Squeeze, Please

How does the bolus travel down the esophagus? It doesn't just drop down— it has some help. The bolus is pushed down the esophagus, little by little, by waves of muscle contractions, called peristalsis. Muscles of the esophagus contract, or squeeze. This moves the bolus down the esophagus in about three to four seconds. Then the bolus goes through a ring of muscles called a sphincter, which opens to let food enter the stomach. The sphincter at the bottom of the esophagus is called the lower esophageal sphincter.

MUSCLE CONTRACTS

ESOPHAGUS

BOLUS

MUSCLE RELAXES

THIS IS KIND OF FUN!

LOWER ESOPHAGE SPHINCT

STOMACH

14

So, What's Up with Belching?

All sphincters in the body act like doors, letting things go through one way, just a little at a time. Food and liquid go through the lower esophageal sphincter to the stomach. When you drink certain things such as soda, air can get into your stomach. When this happens, that air can travel backward through the lower esophageal sphincter and up the esophagus. The next thing you may hear is a burp, or belch. Oh . . . excuse me.

HOW RUDE!

BLAAAP!

Belching Cola

Upset Stomach?

Now the bolus is in the amazing stomach. You might think, *What's so amazing about the stomach?* It's just an organ where your food goes, right? Well, there's a lot more to the stomach than meets the eye: gastric juices are produced here, stomach muscles churn, and chyme is made here.

ESOPHAGUS

BOLUS

YOU CALL **THIS** A PARTY?

There's quite a party going on, but how does the stomach use all this stuff?

SMALL INTESTINE

We Have Such Chemistry

The stomach digests food chemically. Different cells in the stomach wall, or lining, make different chemicals, called gastric juices, that help break down food. Some cells make enzymes, some cells make acid, and other cells make mucus.

A stomach enzyme called pepsin breaks down proteins in foods such as meat. Pepsin needs acid around it in order to work. But where are you going to get acid in your stomach? Luckily there are cells in your stomach that make hydrochloric acid, which is so strong it could burn a hole in this book!

Wait a minute. Why doesn't this acid burn a hole in your stomach lining? Well, your stomach makes something cool that protects its lining. What's our hero? It's mucus. Without it, your stomach would be in a lot of trouble . . . and so would you. Actually, hydrochloric acid is a hero too, because it kills some of the germs that might be in the foods you eat.

As the Stomach Churns

Your stomach is also quite strong. Well, it couldn't beat you at arm wrestling, but it has muscles that squeeze or churn. This action makes food smaller. It's like you're working out while you eat.

PANT PANT

Make Time for Chyme

Chewing, churning, and chemicals . . . oh my! Food has been broken down a lot at this point. In fact, by the time food leaves the stomach, it kind of looks like melted ice cream. This partially digested food and acid mixture is called chyme.

What's Up...Chuck?

When everything is working right in the stomach, you might not think about things like acid and mucus. But if a virus makes you sick, food can go out the wrong way. Yes, vomiting is very unpleasant, but it's the body's way of getting rid of invaders. It can even cause a burning feeling in the esophagus because of the acid that comes up with the food. Okay, I'm sorry I brought up that subject!

In order to leave the stomach the right way, food goes through another sphincter, called the pyloric sphincter, into the next fascinating place: the small intestine.

Diving into the Small Intestine

The small intestine is where the job of digestion is finished. This organ looks like a coiled-up tube and measures about one inch in diameter. Does it really need to be coiled up? Well, consider this: the small intestine is about 20 feet long. That's much longer than you are tall. So, in order for it to fit inside your body, it must be coiled.

The small intestine is split into three sections: the duodenum, the jejunum, and the ileum. It's a very busy place. The body sends in assistance from all over to help finish the job of digesting chyme.

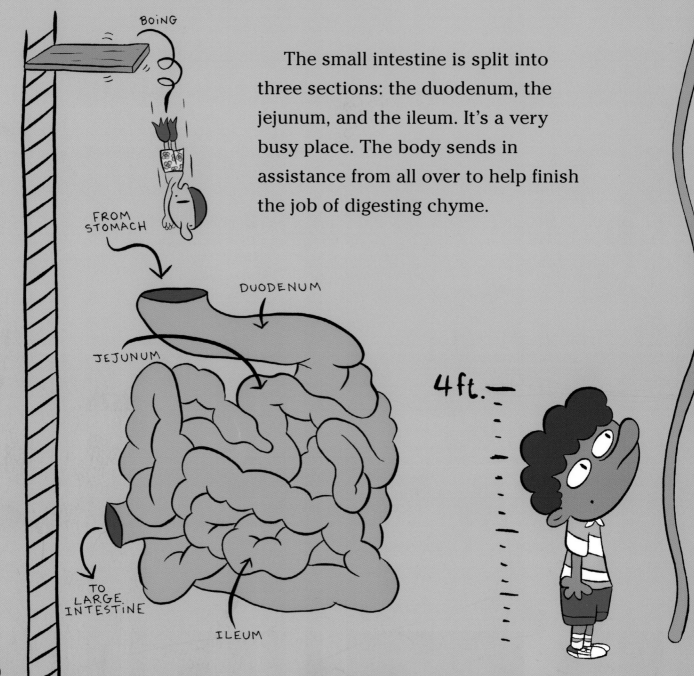

BOING

FROM STOMACH

DUODENUM

JEJUNUM

4 ft. —

TO LARGE INTESTINE

ILEUM

20

Lending a Hand

The pancreas—a nearby gland—sends over enzymes to digest carbohydrates, proteins, and fats. The liver lends a hand by making bile, which is then stored in the gallbladder until it's time to go to the small intestine.

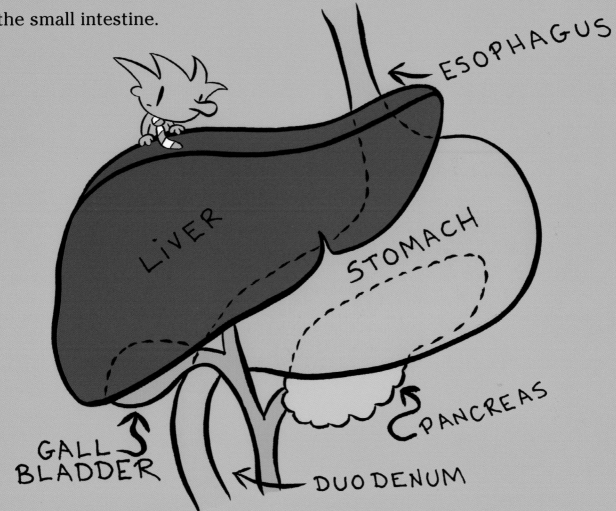

THIS IS HARD WORK.

BILE

SPLAT!

FATS

Bile's job is to help break down fats. Needless to say, the small intestine is a digester's dream come true.

Happy Cells

The body has done a great job of digesting food so far. So now what does the body do with all those tiny food particles? After the big party in the duodenum, tiny food particles are absorbed by or pass through the small intestine's lining and go into the bloodstream. If the food is not absorbed in the duodenum, it can still be absorbed later, in the jejunum or the ileum.

Let's get even closer . . . closer. . . . Food moves around in the small intestine, stirred by fingerlike nutrient-absorbing projections in the intestinal wall called villi. Those tiny food particles go through the villi before they pass into the blood vessels of the small intestine.

VILLI

BLOOD
VESSELS

Many of these food particles travel through the bloodstream and are delivered to the body's cells. The "happy" little cells now have food to use in a cool chemical reaction called cellular respiration. Oxygen, which came in at the lungs, has also been delivered to the cells at this point. Food, oxygen, and water in the cells react. This reaction—cellular respiration—produces carbon dioxide, water, and most importantly . . . energy! This energy can be used for bodily functions such as making your heart beat, breathing, repairing cells, and even digesting your food!

A Large Help

Wait a minute! It's great that we get energy from all this, but what happens to stuff we eat that doesn't go to cells? Well, if your body doesn't digest it and can't use it, you get rid of it. Just like we put things we can't use in a garbage can, our body puts stuff it can't use, or wastes, into the large intestine.

At five feet long, the large intestine is actually shorter than the small intestine. But the large intestine gets its big name because it's wider than the small intestine.

Wastes travel from the small intestine to the large intestine's cecum, ascending colon, transverse colon, descending colon, and sigmoid colon and finally to the rectum and anus.

TRANSVERSE COLON

ASCENDING COLON

DESCENDING COLON

Some important things happen to wastes as they travel through the large intestine. When they arrive in the cecum, wastes are very liquidy. But not for long. Water is "recycled," or reabsorbed, from the wastes so your body doesn't lose the water it needs to stay hydrated.

Another thing that happens in the large intestine is that wastes are formed into feces with the help of mucus. Again mucus helps our body by protecting the large intestine as feces prepare to exit the body.

CECUM

ILEUM

APPENDIX

SIGMOID COLON

RECTUM

GOING UP?

ANUS

ANAL SPHINCTER

A Happy Ending

Feces are made mostly of water and undigested foods. Mucus lining the intestinal walls makes it easier for the feces to leave the body. The rectum at the end of the large intestine is the waiting room, where wastes hang out until they can leave the body. The very end of the large intestine, called the anus, includes an opening, which is controlled by sphincter muscles. That's why you have control over when to use the restroom to get rid of these wastes.

Your Little Friends

Another important job of the large intestine is that it's home to some little friends. These friends are helpful bacteria that make vitamin K for you. Vitamin K helps keep your blood healthy.

Bacteria also help to keep things in your large intestine working right. In fact, when the number of these bacteria is lowered, you can get diarrhea, which causes your body to lose water. Wastes come out very liquidy instead of solid. So the next time you feel something happening and hear gurgling in your intestine, get ready . . . it may be "the runs."

If some undigested food makes it to your large intestine, it might be eaten or digested by these bacteria. You might think, *What's the harm?* They help me; I can give them a little food, right? Well, in return for the food, the bacteria give you something . . . gas. They sometimes produce smelly gases known as flatulence.

WAS THAT YOU?

NO, IT WAS THE BACTERIA IN MY LARGE INTESTINE.

From Start to Finish

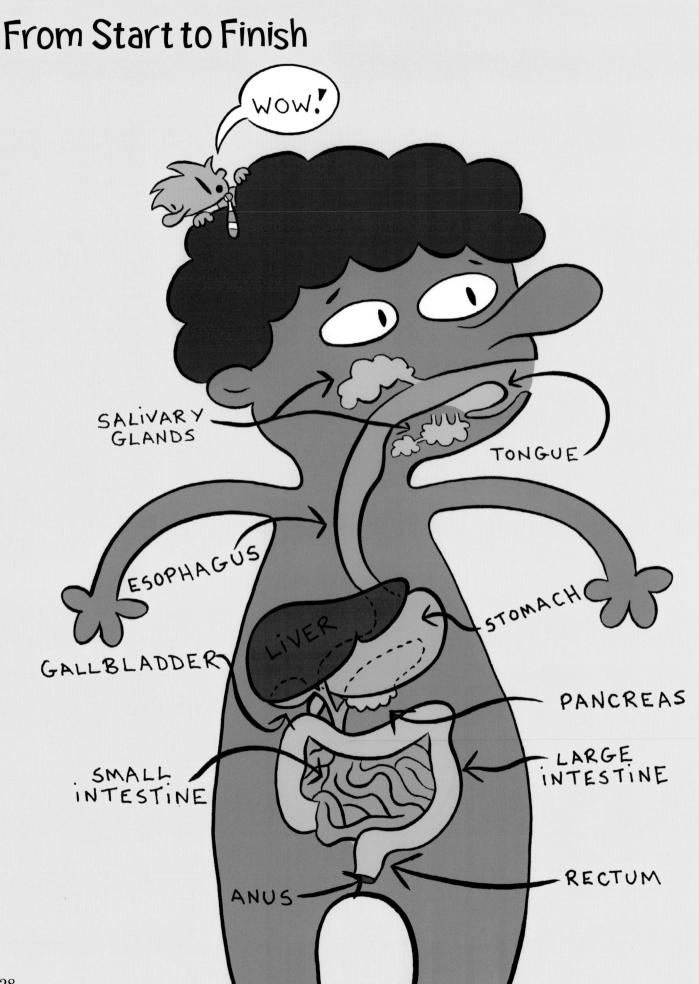

So, in a nutshell, digestion is a cool (but sometimes gross) process that breaks down the food you eat. Some nutrients can then go to body cells to take part in bodily functions. What you can't use leaves the body as waste.

BUT I'M STILL HUNGRY.

GRUMBLE

GRUMBLE

The End

So, let's hear it for digestion— because you couldn't be at your best without the quest to digest!

Glossary

anus (AY-nus): The opening at the end of the large intestine, through which feces leave the body.

bacterium (bak-TEER-ee-um): A one-celled living organism. Some bacteria are helpful to humans, while others are harmful. (plural: bacteria)

bile (BIE-l): A substance made by the liver and stored in the gallbladder. Bile helps break down fats in the small intestine.

bladder (BLAD-er): An organ that stores urine before it leaves the body.

bolus (BOH-lus): A rounded lump of food ready for swallowing.

canine (KAY-nine): One of four pointed teeth that rip and tear food.

carbohydrate (kar-boh-HIE-drayt): A substance in food that is made up of carbon, hydrogen, and oxygen. Carbohydrates include sugars and starches. They provide energy.

cecum (SEE-kum): The first section of the large intestine.

cell (SEL): The basic structure of living things. Cells need food, oxygen, and water in order to function and stay alive.

cellular respiration (SEL-yew-ler res-puh-RAY-shun): The chemical reaction in which oxygen, water, and glucose (a kind of sugar found in food) react to produce water, carbon dioxide, and energy.

chyme (KIME): Once a bolus has been digested in the stomach, it is then called chyme.

colon (KO-lin): The second section, and the biggest part, of the large intestine.

diarrhea (die-uh-REE-uh): Watery feces.

digestion (die-JEHST-shun): A process by which food is broken down so it can be absorbed by the body.

duodenum (doo-uh-DEE-num, also pronounced doo-AW-den-um): The first section of the small intestine.

enzymes (EN-zimes): Proteins that assist with chemical reactions in the body. Enzymes are necessary for cells to function and act as catalysts for chemical reactions.

epiglottis (eh-puh-GLAW-tis): A flap that covers the trachea when food is swallowed. This prevents the food from going down the trachea and causing the person to choke.

esophagus (ih-SAW-fuh-gus): A muscular tube that carries food from the pharynx to the stomach.

feces (FEE-seez): Solid wastes, also called bowel movements.

flatulence (FLAT-chuh-lents): Gas formed in the stomach or intestine that leaves the body through the anus.

gallbladder (GAWL-blad-er): A small sac near the liver that stores bile.

gastric juice (GAS-trik JOOS): A chemical made in the stomach that helps break down food.

hard palate (HARD PAL-ut): The bony part of the roof of the mouth located near the front teeth. The tongue presses food against the hard palate when food is being chewed.

hydrated (HIE-dray-ted): Having enough water in the body to be healthy and to maintain bodily functions.

hydrochloric acid (hie-droh-KLAWR-ik ASS-id): A strong acid produced in the stomach that helps in the digestive process.

ileum (IH-lee-um): The last section of the small intestine.

incisor (in-SIE-zer): One of eight teeth found in the front of the mouth that cut foods.

jejunum (jih-JOO-num): The middle section of the small intestine.

kidney (KID-nee): One of a pair of organs that help filter waste from the blood and send this waste to the bladder in the form of urine.

large intestine (LAWRJ in-TES-tun): The body organ in which wastes are prepared to leave the body.

liver (LIH-ver): A large organ that does many jobs, including making bile.

molar (MOH-ler): One of twelve flat or rounded teeth in the back of the mouth that grind and chew food.

mucus (MYOO-kus): A sticky, slimy substance produced by the body. Mucus protects and lubricates body parts such as the mouth, nose, and stomach.

nutrient (NOO-tree-ent): A substance that the body needs in order to survive and be healthy. Proteins, carbohydrates, and vitamins are examples of nutrients.

palate (PAL-ut): The roof of the mouth.

pancreas (PANG-kree-us): A gland that makes digestive enzymes, as well as insulin. Insulin keeps the right amount of sugar in the blood.

pepsin (PEP-sun): An enzyme made in the stomach that helps break down proteins.

peristalsis (pehr-uh-STAWL-sis): Wavelike contractions that move food through the esophagus and the intestines.

pharynx (FEH-ringks): The area of the throat between the mouth and the esophagus.

protein (PROH-teen): A substance containing carbon, oxygen, hydrogen, and nitrogen that makes up the basic structural material of the body. Proteins also include enzymes.

rectum (REK-tum): The last section of the large intestine. Wastes are stored in the rectum until they leave the body through the anus.

saliva (suh-LIE-vuh): The liquid in the mouth made by salivary glands. Saliva contains mucus, water, and digestive enzymes that begin to break down food.

small intestine (SMAWL in-TES-tun): The body organ in which digestion is complete, and where nutrients are absorbed into the bloodstream.

soft palate: (SAWFT PAL-ut): The muscular area of the roof of the mouth that separates the hard palate and the pharynx. The uvula hangs from the bottom of the soft palate.

sphincter (SFIHNGK-tuhr): A ring of muscles that opens and closes to allow a certain amount of substance, for example food, through at a time. There are sphincters located at the top and bottom of the esophagus as well as in other places of the body.

trachea (TRAY-kee-uh): The windpipe. A tubelike structure that starts near the epiglottis and runs into the lungs. Air is cleaned as it passes through the trachea.

urine (YER-in): Liquid waste made by the kidneys that is stored in the bladder.

uvula (YOOV-yuh-luh): The little piece of flesh that hangs down in the back of the throat. The uvula works with the soft palate to cover the nasal passages and prevent food from entering these passages during swallowing.

villus (VIH-lus): A small, fingerlike projection through which food particles travel to reach the bloodstream. (plural: villi)

virus (VIE-rus): Any of a number of small "invaders" that can get into the body and cause diseases, such as the common cold. They invade cells in order to reproduce.

vitamin K (VIE-tih-min KAY): A vitamin that helps blood to clot.

For more information about digestion, check out these websites.

Human Anatomy Online
http://www.innerbody.com/htm/body.html
This site, sponsored by
www.myhealthsource.com,
offers information about various body
systems. After choosing a system,
readers can learn more about each
organ and its function by highlighting
the diagram with the cursor.

KidsHealth
http://www.kidshealth.org/kid/
A helpful resource for kids that covers
numerous topics, including health,
illnesses, and growing up. The Game
Closet features short videos about bodily
functions, including the digestive system.

Enchanted Learning
http://www.EnchantedLearning.com/subjects
/anatomy/digestive/index.shtml
Find out more about the digestive system
at this website. There's a glossary of
important terms, and readers can print
out the human digestive system diagram.

For further reading, here are some more books to digest!

Parker, Steve. *Digestion*. Chicago, IL:
Raintree, 2004.
Walker, Richard, ed. *Encyclopedia of the
Human Body*. New York: DK Publishing,
2002.
Walker, Richard, et. al. *Under the Microscope:
The Human Body*. Danbury, CT: Grolier
Educational, 1998.

Bibliography

Gray, Henry. *Anatomy of the Human Body*,
30th edition. Philadelphia, PA: Lea &
Febiger, 1985.

Marieb, Elaine N. *Anatomy & Physiology*. San
Francisco, CA: Benjamin Cummings, 2002.

Starr, Cecie. *Biology: The Unity and Diversity
of Life*, 5th edition. Belmont, CA:
Wadsworth Publishing Company, 1989.